better together*

*This book is best read together, grownup and kid.

 akidsco.com

a
kids
book
about

a kids book about

adventure

by Dr. Ben Tertin

A Kids Co.
Editor and Designer Jelani Memory
Creative Director Rick DeLucco
Studio Manager Kenya Feldes
Sales Director Melanie Wilkins
Head of Books Jennifer Goldstein
CEO and Founder Jelani Memory

DK
Editor Emma Roberts
Senior Production Editor Jennifer Murray
Senior Production Controller Louise Minihane
Senior Acquisitions Editor Katy Flint
Managing Art Editor Vicky Short
Publishing Director Mark Searle

This American Edition, 2024
Published in the United States by DK Publishing
1745 Broadway, 20th Floor, New York, NY 10019

DK, a Division of Penguin Random House LLC
Cover by Jonathon Simcoe

A catalog record for this book is available from the Library of Congress.
ISBN: 978-0-7440-9465-7

DK books are available at special discounts when purchased in bulk for
sales promotions, premiums, fund-raising, or educational use. For details, contact:
DK Publishing Special Markets, 1745 Broadway, 20th Floor, New York, NY 10019, or SpecialSales@dk.com

Printed and bound in China

www.dk.com

akidsco.com

This book was made with Forest
Stewardship Council™ certified
paper - one small step in DK's
commitment to a sustainable future.
**For more information go to
www.dk.com/our-green-pledge**

For Annabelle and Wesley,
my beloved.

Intro
for grownups

As a parent, I instinctively want to give comfort and security to my kids. I want to protect them from failure and pain. And yet, I'm learning that this good, instinctive desire to keep them cozy can actually do them harm.

When I teach them to wonder, risk, attempt, learn, and grow, then I am teaching them how to open up and come alive.

However, when I teach them to chase comfort and security, I shut them off from reality. Worse, rather than helping them learn to live, I merely teach them to get through their days safely.

Deep down, we grownups want to help unpredictable little miracles explode into beautiful lives. We want to help develop and nurture an adventurous spirit within them.

That's why I wrote this book.

Once upon a time...

Just kidding! This is not that kind of story.

adventure.

My name is Ben.

I grew up in a small family in a little town that had a HUGE chocolate factory.

Really, it did...
and the whole town often smelled like cocoa.

My sister and I rode bikes and scooters and skateboards every day. We caught fish and frogs in the river. We played with our brown dog, Zeke, and built forts and swings in the woods.

Oh, and we picked lots of raspberries too.

Sometimes enough to make a pie!

Our town,
our home,
our street,
our woods,
our river,
and even the warm chocolate
smell in the air, was all familiar.

Most days, we knew just
what to expect.

That felt good.

Really
good!

But **then**

we   moved.

To a new state.
To a new city.
To a new house.
To a new school.
To a new EVERYTHING.

Guess what I felt inside...

Afraid!

Do you ever feel afraid when you face something new?

Of course you do!
We ALL do.

Why?

Because we don't know what to expect.

We don't know what is going to happen.

But, check this out:

NOT KNOWING WHAT WILL HAPPEN is the secret to *adventure.*

Here's the deal:

We ~~like~~ LOVE to know what is going to happen.

When things are familiar, it feels good.

But we get ~~worried~~ TERRIFIED when we don't know what will happen.

That kind of worry is OK because it helps you pay attention to real danger.

Adventure
does not mean being
careless or **foolish.**

Adventure

means being smart and learning the difference between true danger and what is good.

When something is new, we quickly ask...

What if it doesn't work out?

What if they don't like me?

What if it tastes like onions?

What if I don't win?

What if they laugh at me?

What if this ends up
making me cry?

**All because we're afraid of
what might happen.**

Sometimes we worry about new schools, new towns, new teams, new foods, or even new families.

Sometimes we worry about big things, like flying in an airplane, or learning to swim in deep water.

Sometimes small things, like reading new books, or going to new places, can make us worry.

YIKES! THERE ARE SO MANY NEW THINGS!*

*This book might even be new!

So, what can you do?

Remember, the secret to *adventure* **is NOT KNOWING WHAT WILL HAPPEN.**

**When you don't know
what will happen,**

and you feel that normal worry,

**go ahead and think through
the bad things that
could happen,**

but also WONDER about
the good things.

Instead of only asking,

"What if I fail?"
OR,
"What if this ends poorly?",

you can ask,

"Why not try?"
OR,
"Why not see if this ends well?"

Like...

Why not try to make a
new friend?

Why not try to discover
something new about yourself
or the world around you?

Why not try to learn a new
sport, instrument, or
game with friends?

Saying,

"OK. Why not?"

can help you come up with a million good things to hope for instead of a million bad things to worry about...

BECAUSE ARE SO GOOD THAT

THERE MANY THINGS CAN HAPPEN!

Adventure

means being willing to try something new... growing healthy and strong as you do.

So, try to remember these 2 words:

1. Why
2. Not?

New things come up all the time, and you will worry (that's normal).

Remember to ask, "Why not?" and wonder about how this new thing might be awesome.

**When you do that,
you are headed for great**
adventure.

From a guy
who grew up
building tree forts
and rope swings in a
little town that smelled
like chocolate, I say to you...
May your life be full of endless

nture.

Why not?

The End.

Outro
for grownups

Is adventure risky? Yes. Is it comfortable and secure? No, and no.

Encourage your kiddo to take risks and do new things, because that's where true adventure happens.

Here are some fun things to try:

1. Remind them of a time when they didn't want to try something new, but it ended up being amazing.

2. Tell them about a time when you were worried about some new thing and didn't try it because you asked "What if?" instead of "Why not?"

3. Challenge them to try 1 new thing TODAY! Something they would have said no to yesterday, but might be willing to try now.

Help them find a new adventure every day, and, just maybe, you'll find one too!

About The Author

Dr. Ben Tertin (he/him) wrote this book to help kids move through fear by embracing honest curiosity. Growing up, Ben frequently changed schools and experienced the trauma of violence in his home, which led to crippling fear. His "safe place" became the forests, rivers, and lakes around the places he lived, and it is here that he experienced an increased love for discovery.

In this book, he talks frankly about scary experiences and helps strengthen young people—kids facing big changes, kids moving to new places, or kids feeling scared or overwhelmed by whatever is on the horizon. Love for adventure has brought healing for Ben, and he hopes to help others (kids and grownups) overcome their own fears by embracing the same kind of love for new experiences and good adventures.

 @bentertin    @Ben.Tertin

Made to empower.

a kids book about racism
by Jelani Memory

a kids book about ANXIETY
by Ross Szabo

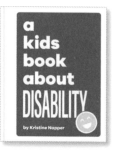
a kids book about DISABILITY
by Kristine Napper

a kids book about IMAGINATION
by LEVAR BURTON

a kids book about belonging
by Kevin Carroll

a kids book about failyure
by Dr. Laymon Hicks

a kids book about GRATITUDE
by Ben Kenyon

a kids book about LIFE ONLINE
by Dave S. Anderson & Blake Fleischacker

a kids book about body image
by Rebecca Alexander

a kids book about IMMIGRATION
by MJ Calderon

a kids book about EMPATHY
by Daron K. Roberts

a kids book about GENDER
by Dale Mueller

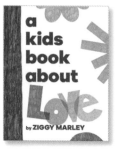
a kids book about Love
by ZIGGY MARLEY

a kids book about EQUALITY
by BILLIE JEAN KING

a kids book about MONEY
by Adam Stramwasser

a kids book about FEMINISM
by Emma McIlroy

a kids book about adventure
by Dr. Ben Tertin

a kids book about CLIMATE CHANGE
by Zanagee Artis & Olivia Greenspan

a kids book about CONFIDENCE
by Joy Cho

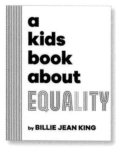
a kids book about BEING NON-BINARY
by Hunter Chinn-Raicht

Discover more at akidsco.com